D0347499

For Zoom Rockman – K. L.
To Mum and Dad – E. G.

Little Genius: Brains
A RED FOX BOOK 978 0 099 45162 4

First published in Great Britain by Hutchinson,
an imprint of Random House Children's Books

Hutchinson edition published 2006
Red Fox edition published 2007

1 3 5 7 9 10 8 6 4 2

Text copyright © Kate Lennard, 2006
Illustrations copyright © Eivind Gulliksen, 2006

The right of Kate Lennard and Eivind Gulliksen to be identified as the author and illustrator of this work has been asserted in accordance with the Copyright, Designs and Patents Act 1988.

All rights reserved.

The Random House Group Limited makes every effort to ensure that the papers used in its books are made from trees that have been legally sourced from well-managed and credibly certified forests. Our paper procurement policy can be found at: www.randomhouse.co.uk/paper.htm

Red Fox Books are published by Random House Children's Books,
61–63 Uxbridge Road, London W5 5SA

www.**kidsatrandomhouse**.co.uk

Addresses for companies within The Random House Group Limited can be found at: www.randomhouse.co.uk/offices.htm

THE RANDOM HOUSE GROUP Limited Reg. No. 954009

A CIP catalogue record for this book is available from the British Library

Printed in China

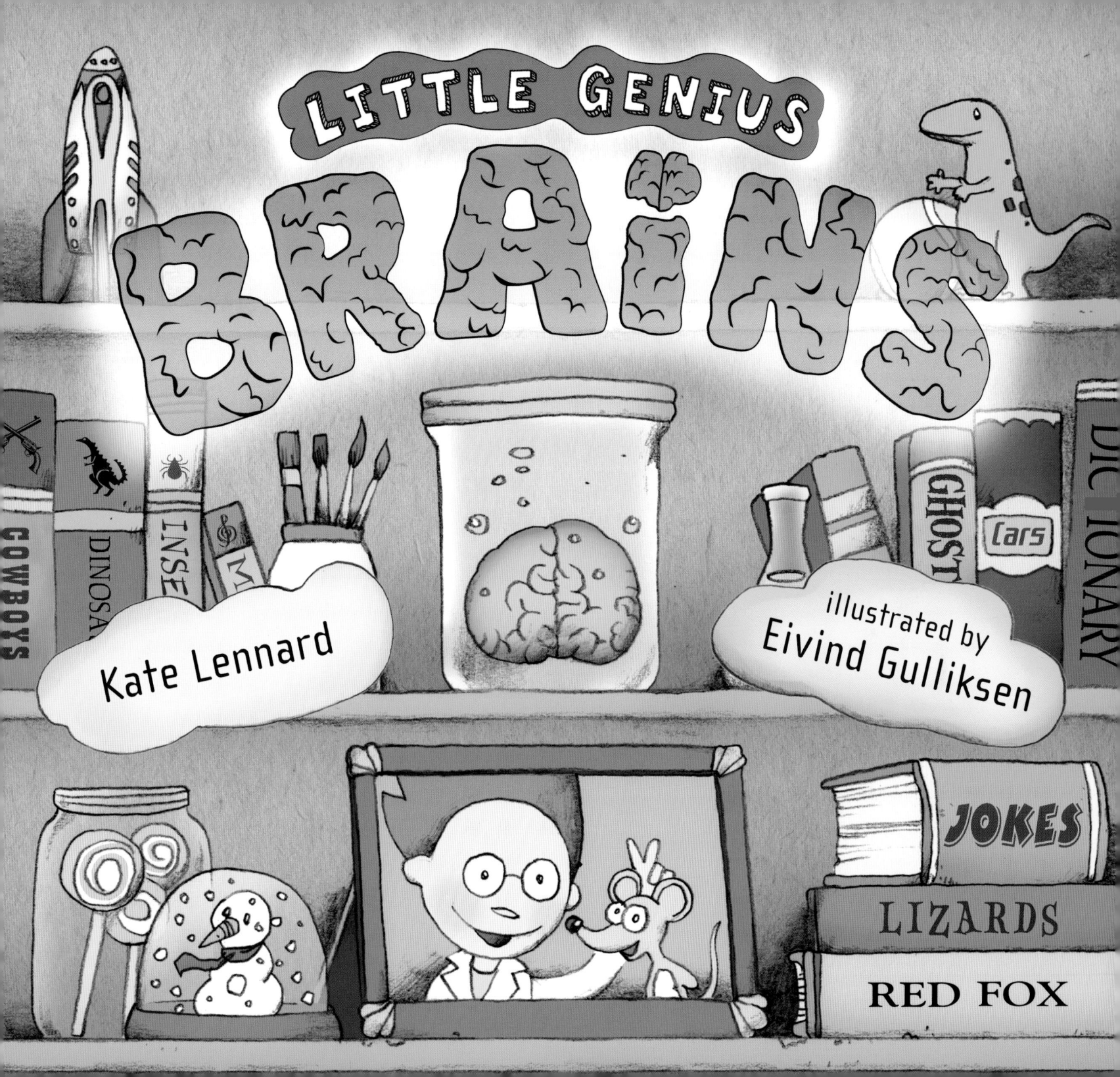
LITTLE GENIUS
BRAINS
COWBOYS
DINOSA
INSE
GHOST
Cars
DIC IONARY
Kate Lennard
illustrated by
Eivind Gulliksen
JOKES
LIZARDS
RED FOX

Little
Genius

Hello!
I'm **Little Genius**.
I've been looking into the human body, and all the interesting bits that make it work.
This book is about the amazing machine inside your head called your
brain.
I'm here to tell you all about it . . .

Inside your head,
behind your eyes,
is an amazing machine
called your **brain.**

Your brain
has a wiggly,
wrinkled surface.

If you could touch your brain,
it would feel wet and wobbly,
like a **big pink jelly**.

Jelly can squash really easily . . .

But you have a strong case
made of bone
to keep your brain safe.
It's called your
skull.

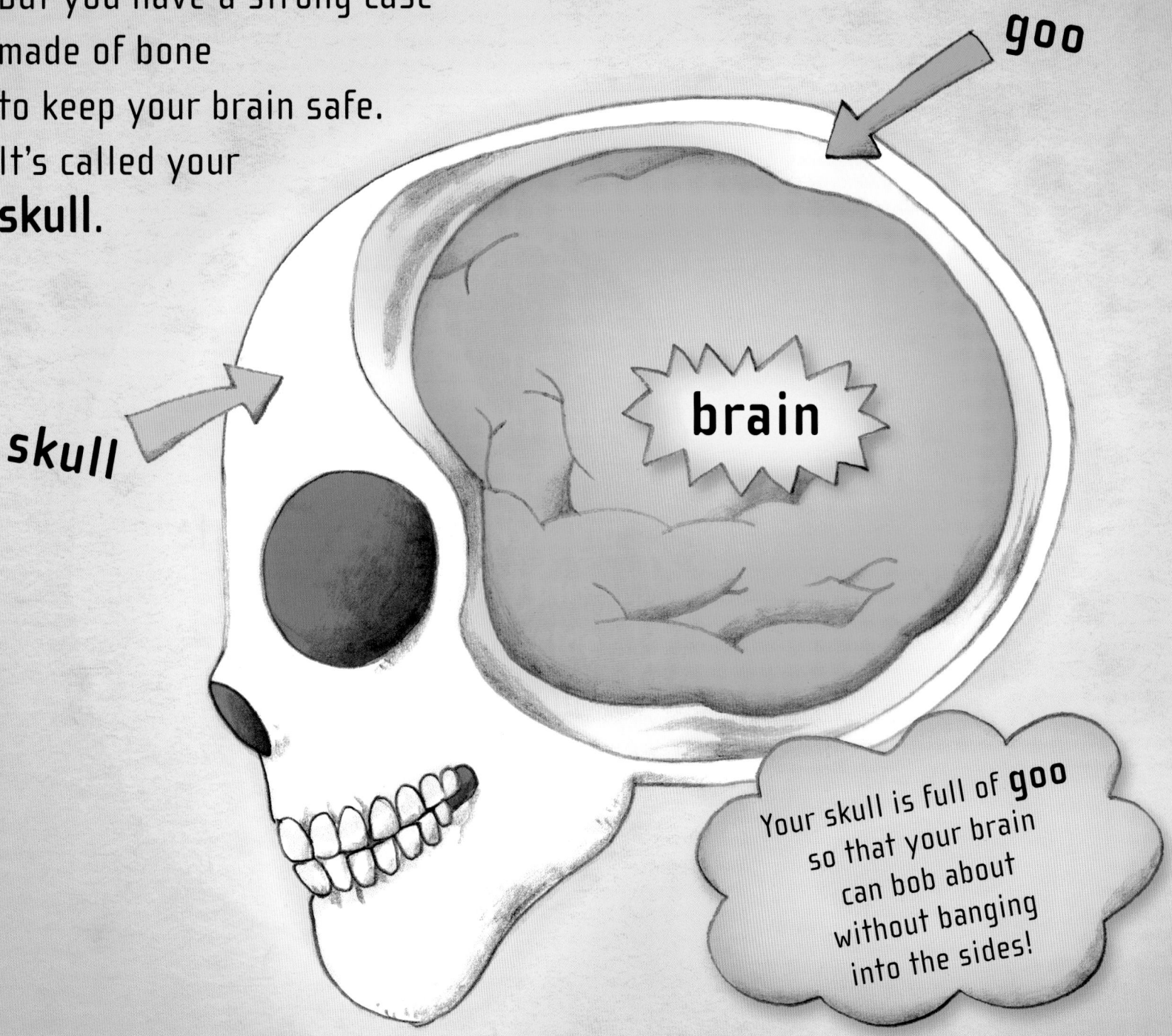

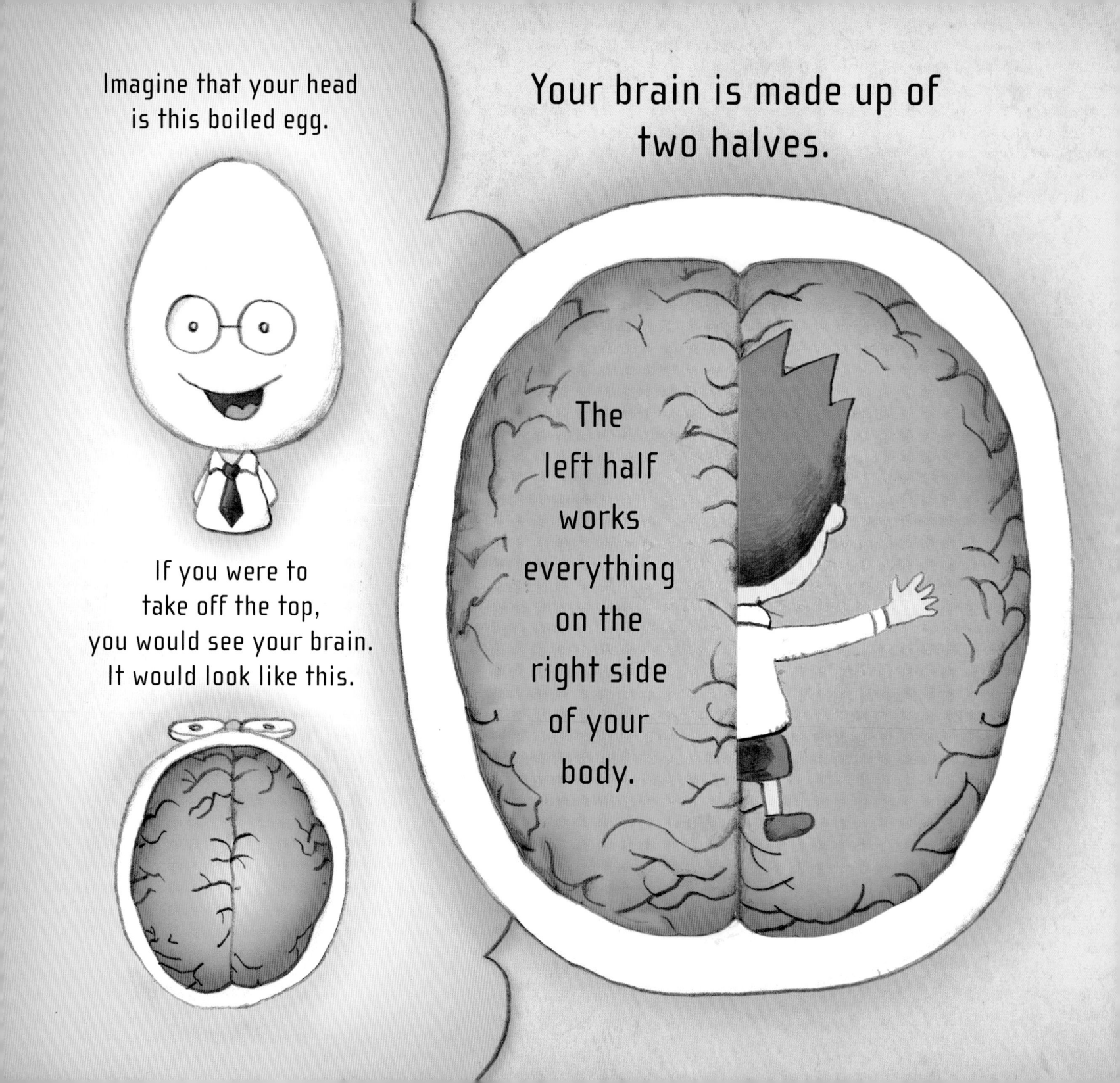
Imagine that your head is this boiled egg.
If you were to take off the top, you would see your brain. It would look like this.
Your brain is made up of two halves.
The left half works everything on the right side of your body.

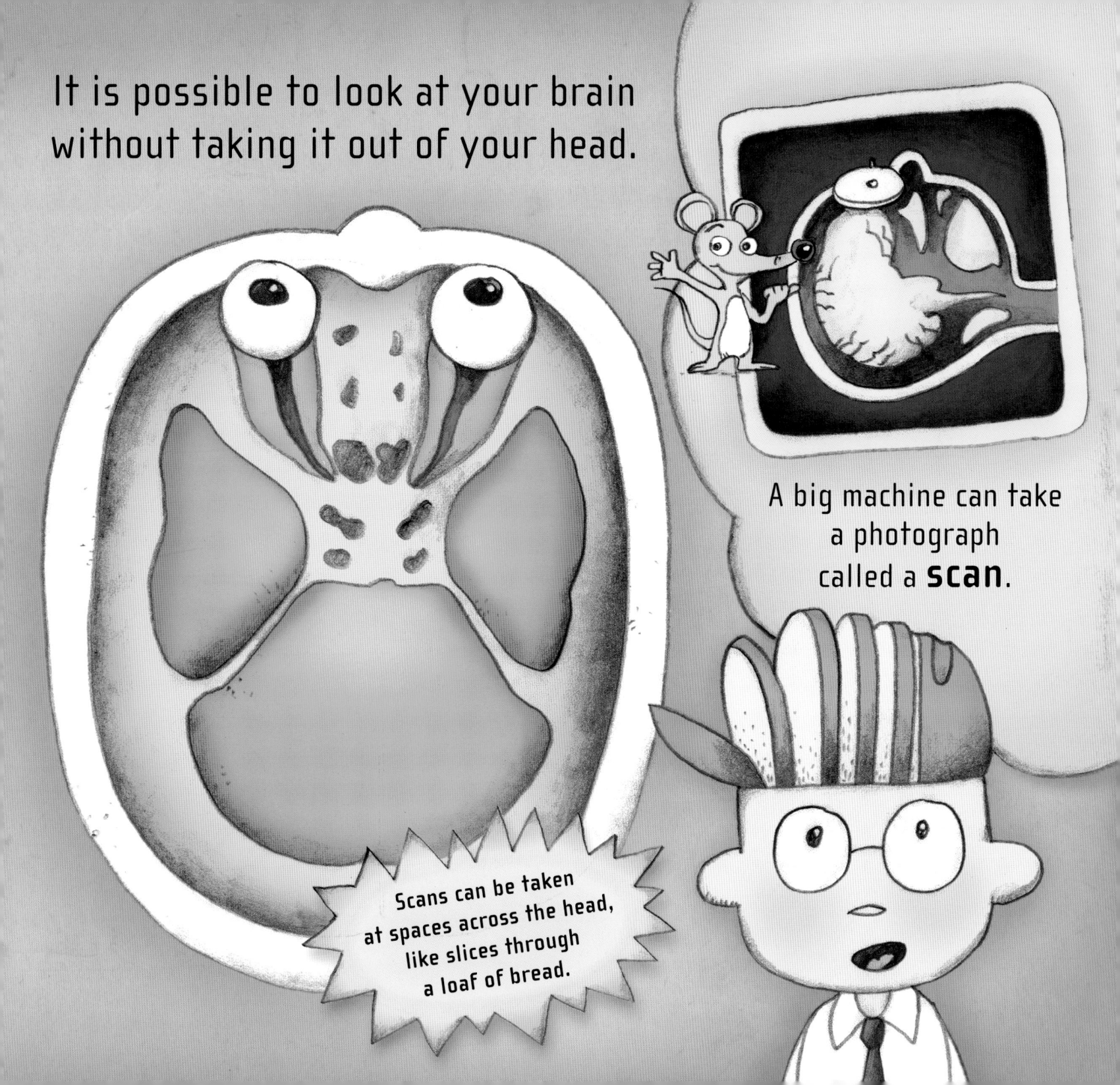
It is possible to look at your brain without taking it out of your head.
A big machine can take a photograph called a **scan**.
Scans can be taken at spaces across the head, like slices through a loaf of bread.

Here is another view of the brain, this time from the side.

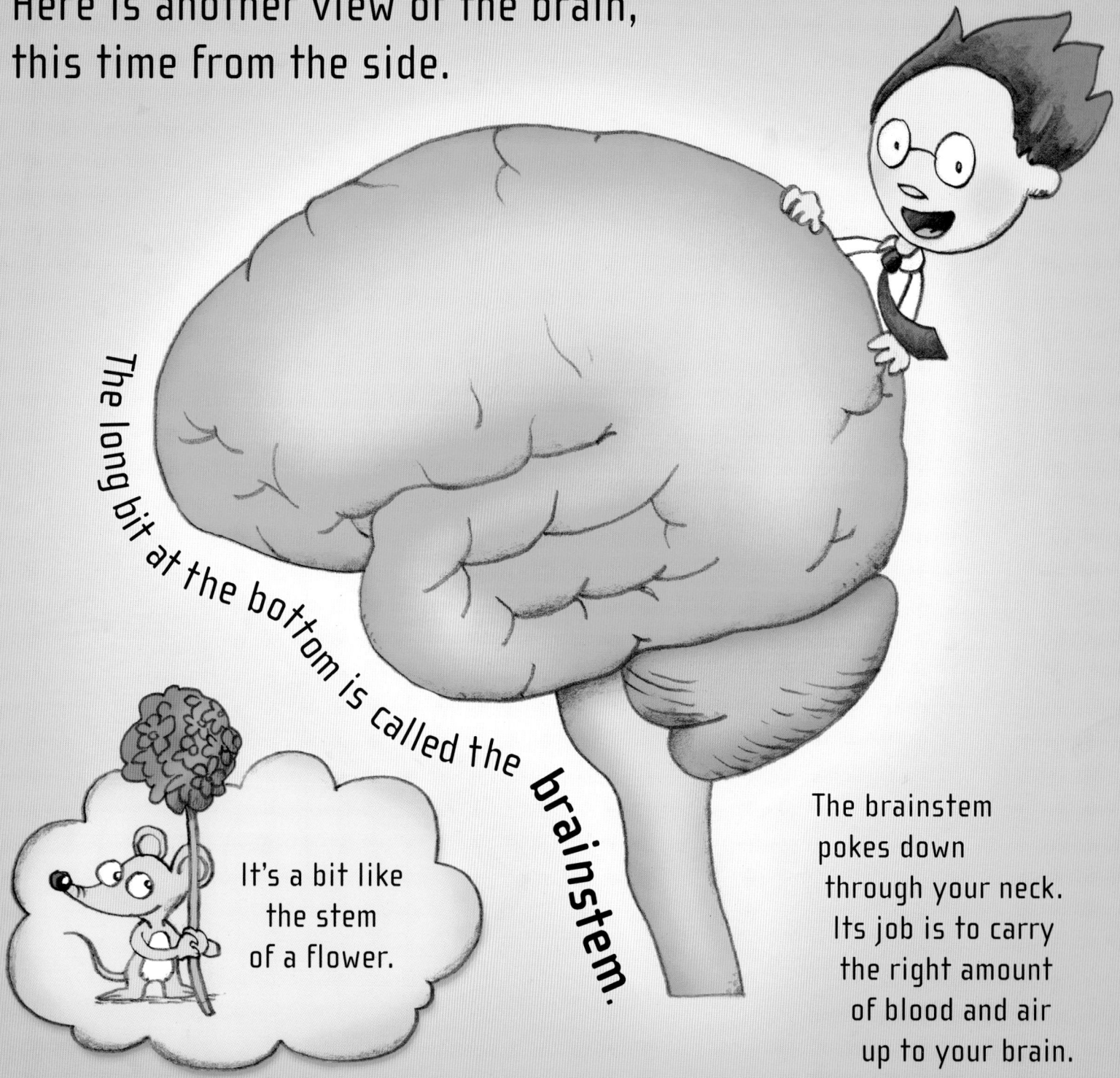

The brainstem pokes down through your neck. Its job is to carry the right amount of blood and air up to your brain.

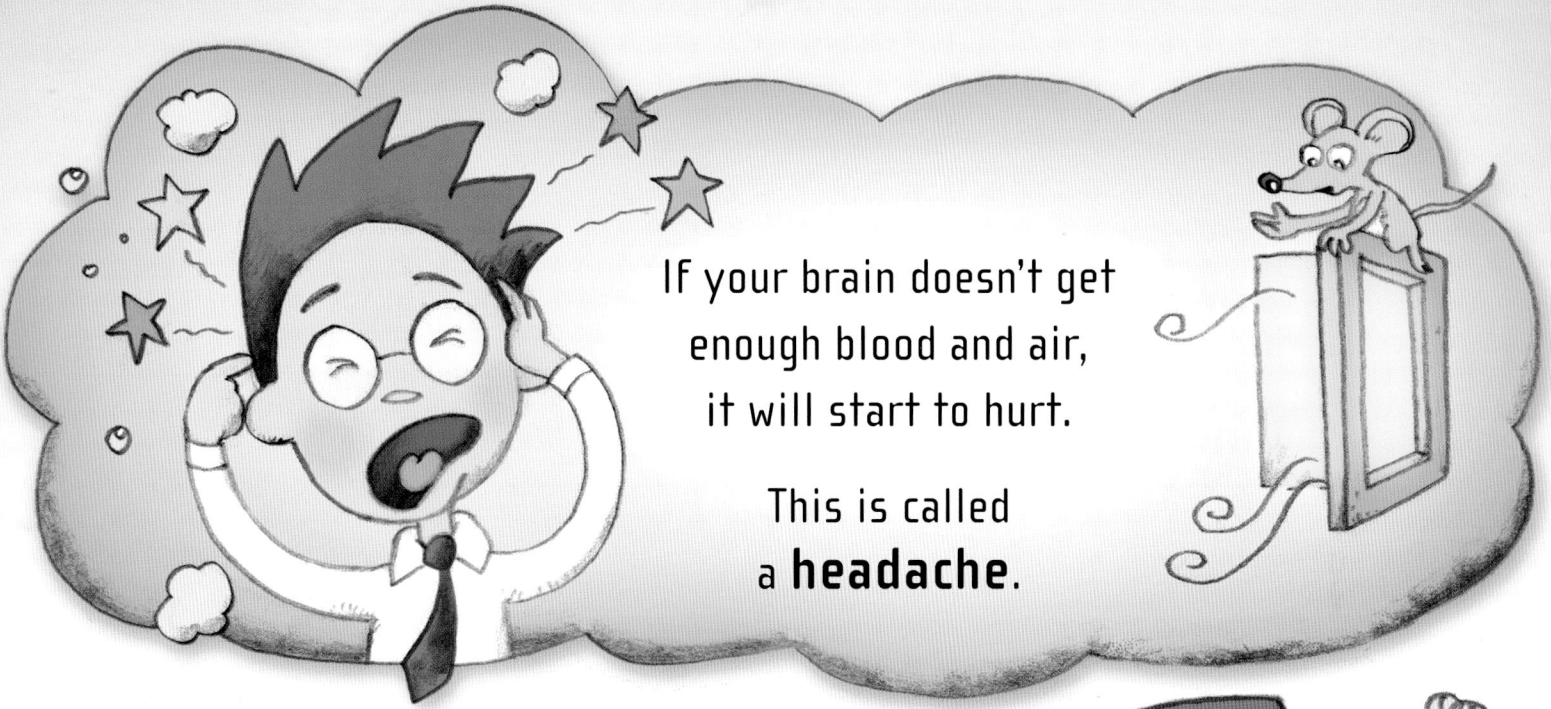

If your brain doesn't get
enough blood and air,
it will start to hurt.

This is called
a **headache**.

You can get
a headache
if you sleep
with your neck
in a funny position
like this.

Every creature has a brain:

Animals with bigger brains aren't always more clever than those with smaller ones.

Humans are very clever.
But other animals are clever too,
like these smart little
dolphins.
They can understand
sign language
and do fantastic tricks.
And they can answer
simple questions like,
Do you want a fish?
or,
Do you want a bucket
on your head?

Dolphins speak to each other by making funny whistling and clicking noises. Unfortunately, nobody knows what they're talking about. So it's hard to find out *just* how clever they are.
We do know that a dolphin can find its way around underwater – even in the darkest places at the bottom of the ocean – like a **submarine**.
Now that is **clever**!
A baby's brain is as heavy as an **apple**.
My brain is as heavy as a **potato**.
A teacher's brain is as heavy as a **pumpkin**.
And a bird's brain is as heavy as half a **pea**!

You use your brain
when you need
to remember something,
like your address
or what you had for breakfast.

If you are trying
to learn something new,
like the name of this planet,
try saying it
over and over again,
closing your eyes
and seeing it as
a picture.
SATURN
BUZZzzzzzz
SATURN is yellow
with amazing stripy rings,
so think of yourself
'sat on' a bumble bee.
That should help
the memory to stick!

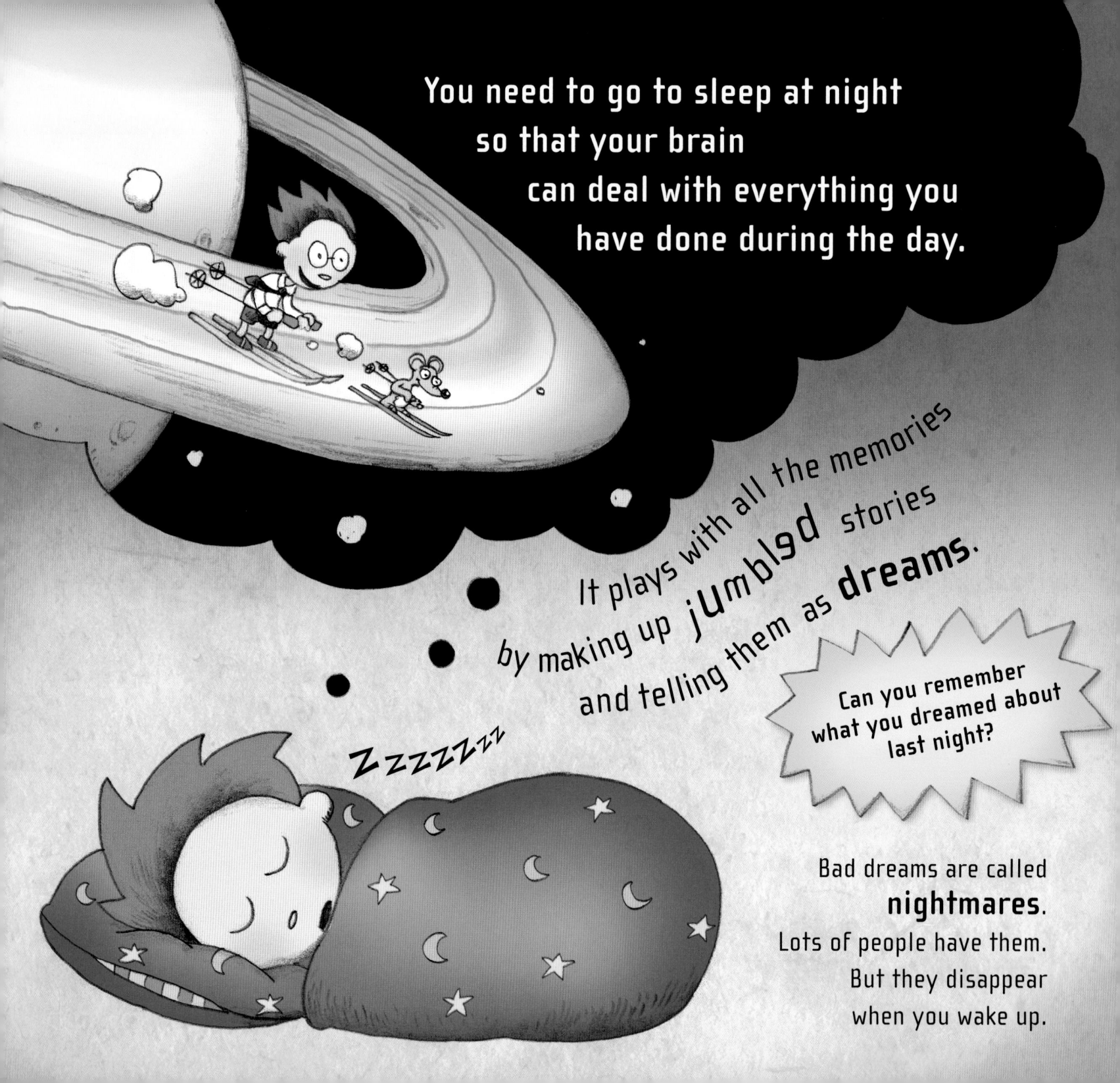
You need to go to sleep at night so that your brain can deal with everything you have done during the day.
It plays with all the memories by making up jumbled stories and telling them as dreams.
Can you remember what you dreamed about last night?
Zzzzzzz
Bad dreams are called nightmares. Lots of people have them. But they disappear when you wake up.

The more you learn,
the quicker your brain will be
at remembering things,
and coming up with answers
to puzzles like these . . .

Sometimes you can picture things in your head that nobody has ever seen before. This is called **imagination**.

Some people are rubbish at puzzles but have brilliant imaginations.

They can think up ideas and tell them as drawings and paintings, or write them as stories.

Reading is very good for your imagination. New words and ideas help your brain grow strong and clever.

Looking

Tasting

Listening

Different parts of the brain are used for different things.

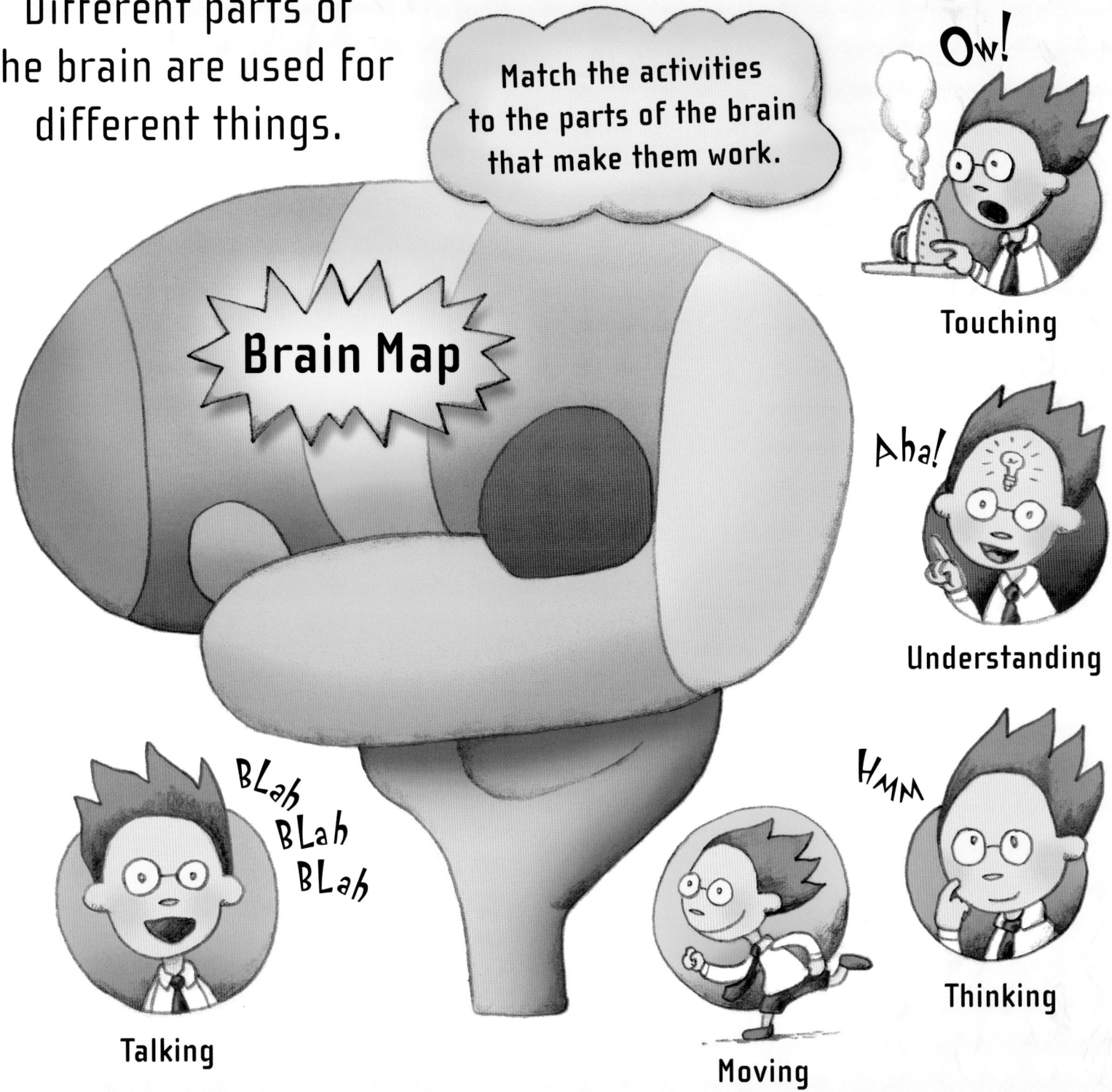

Your brain isn't dry like a football. If you squeezed it you could make **brain juice**! The juice changes flavour depending on what you are doing.
Different kinds of juices make you feel different ways.
A **good** mix of brain juice will make you feel happy and clever.
A **bad** mix of brain juice will make you feel sad and boring.
To make **good brain juice**:
bananas
fish
water
fruit
fresh air
exercise
reading
sleep
hugs
love
laughter

Bad brain juice comes from:
greasy food
smoking
being told off too much
too much telly
or playing on the computer
late nights
spending too much time on your own
This man is not looking after his brain.
The horrible mix of brain juice is tricking him into thinking he needs more bad stuff to stay happy.

A damaged brain can't mend itself like a cut finger.

Some people wear special hats to protect their brains when they are working.

And when they are having fun.

I'm going to really look after my brain.

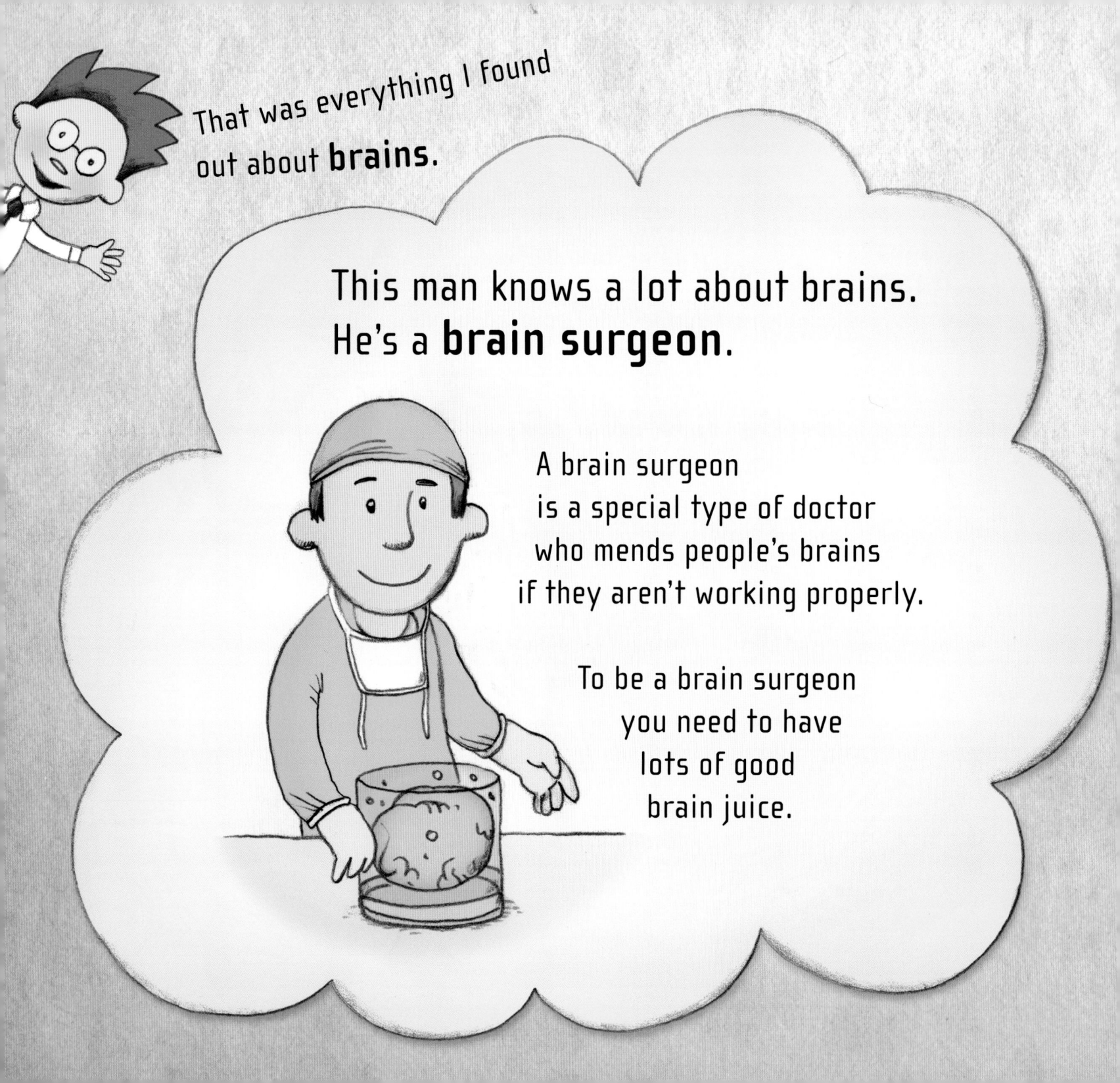
That was everything I found out about **brains**.
This man knows a lot about brains. He's a **brain surgeon**.
A brain surgeon is a special type of doctor who mends people's brains if they aren't working properly.
To be a brain surgeon you need to have lots of good brain juice.

I'd like to be
a brain surgeon
when I grow up.

Would you?

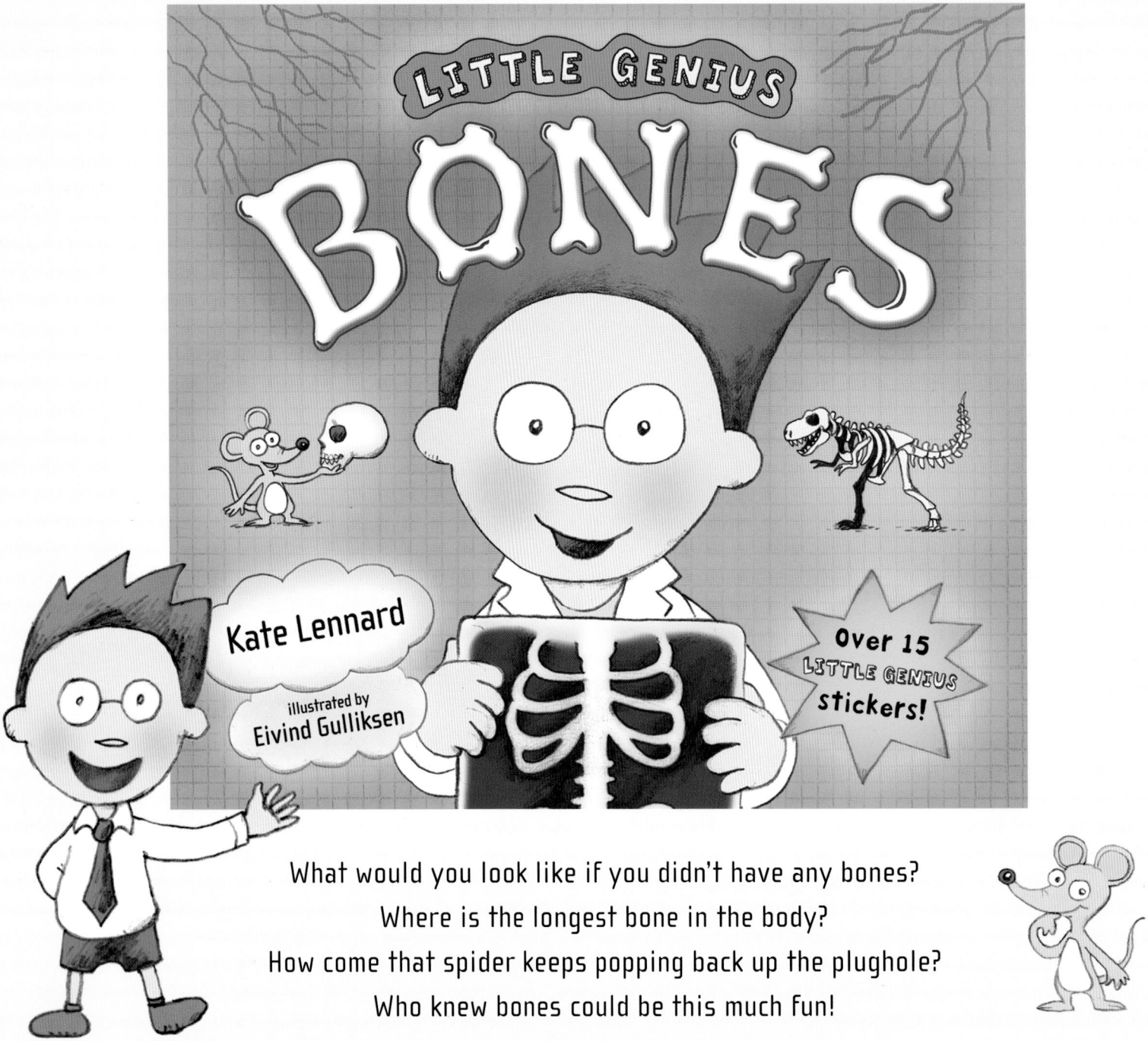

What would you look like if you didn't have any bones?
Where is the longest bone in the body?
How come that spider keeps popping back up the plughole?
Who knew bones could be this much fun!

£4.99 978 0 099 45163 1 Red Fox

RANDOM HOUSE
LIBRARY

I'm a dreamer . . .
I've had a brainwave!
Keep your head!
I've got good brain juice!
Hugs make me grow!
Reading is like taking my brain for a run!
I'm an egg head!
I'm no pea brain!
I've got bad brain juice!
I've had a brainwave!
brain
CE